Warren Buffett

can make you a
millionaire!

Buffett earns

20.8% a year

on average over time

Zhou Wang

Author, **THE Hard Part of Investing:**
Allow your money to work for you

IAN Books

An IAN Books paperback

Published by
IAN Books
41 Watchung Plaza, B242
Montclair, NJ 07042

Cover: Warren Buffett KU by Mark Hirschey

Special sales for educational use by nonprofits.
IANBooksEditor@yahoo.com

1. Investments. 2. Buffett, Warren. I. Wang, Zhou, 1948-. II. Title

332.6--dc21
ISBN-13: 978-1530555987
ISBN-10: 1530555981
Library of Congress Control Number: 2016936026

IAN Books at <u>Amazon.com</u>

Wealth Without Wall Street:
Buy Direct -- Avoid the Commissions, Fees, Loads

The Insiders' Guides to Buying Discount Financial Services:
Buy Direct and Save $3,000 Every Year

Drop Your Insurance:
Buy Only What You Need

Create Financial Freedom Using Your Wealth Reserve™:
Fix your financial life

The Simple Financial Life:
How to get what you want without going into debt and living
paycheck to paycheck

Build Wealth Without Extra Money or Time:
You don't need to budget or get an extra job

Leah's Money Book:
"I want to control my own money."

The Working Millionaire:
$2,000,000 Tax-FREE Wealth Reserve ™ Self-insure Self-fund

Build Your Own $2,000,000 Tax-FREE Wealth Reserve™:
Self-insure Self-fund your lifestyle

Wealth:
What every high school graduate needs to know in the 21st century

Contents

The Warren Buffett phenomenon

$100 invested in 1965 = $1,826,163

"The stock market is a device for transferring money from the
impatient to the patient."

"We continue to make more money when *snoring* than when active."

"My wealth has come from a combination of living in America, some
lucky genes, and **compound interest**."

Mr Buffett's strategy of patience has proven to be the most
astounding in history. He has earned 20.8% a year compounded
over 50 years for his shareholders. His firm had 2 bad years. He
does NOT trade or speculate. He holds companies for a long time.

The **average investor earned just 3.79%** while the stock
market earned 11.06% over the last 30 years. DALBAR Most
investors jump from one "popular" security to another just in time
for them to go down. So they earn just 3.79%; paying more … for
less. Buffett has been patient for over 60 years: his $6,000 from
paper routes has grown to $72 billions.

http://www.fool.com/investing/general/2014/02/07/beat-the-market-with-1-stock.aspx

You and I can become wealthy by buying Buffett's stock. We
don't need to read and understand thousands of company annual
reports. He knows and buys his stocks on sale: Coke, GEICO, Fruit
of the Loom, Benjamin Moore, Acme Bricks, Burlington Northern.
berkshirehathaway.com/ We can't compete but we can be wealthy.

We can earn 20% by buying and holding just one stock:
Buffett's Berkshire Hathaway BRK shares. We don't need to trade
or time our buys and sells. All we have to do is be patient. All we
have to do is "snore" and **do NOTHING.**

Working millionaires don't trade stocks. They don't bet the

ranch on a hot tip. That is gambling. AND it doesn't make you rich unless you have insider information. They don't waste their money on high-fee products that brokers or advisors sell. Patience is all we need to become wealthy over time. We must do ... NOTHING. Absolutely nothing.

Buffett tells us he **buys and holds** the most profitable companies he can find. He beats all the 'professional' money managers. This is against everything we have been told by all the "smart" salespeople on Wall Street. It is counter-intuitive to just leave our money alone. But his strategy works. Smart investors take his advice and buy his firm's stock.

Simplicity is the best way to gain wealth. It is usually less expensive too. No one buys and then sells their businesses quickly Buffett says. We can't compound our earnings by buying and selling profitable companies. Compounding takes time.

If we earn 20% a year on average we will become wealthy too. See page 2, Annual Report. http://www.berkshirehathaway.com/2015ar/2015ar.pdf Each of his shareholders have earned extraordinary returns. Recently, Buffett's gains have only matched the market's gains.

However, wise investors know they will never be able to pick the best securities for the future. Even Buffett has a hard time. But that is OK. Market returns average 11% over time. Our client became wealthy JUST using the market index. See page 23.

Buffett has advised casual investors to use a low-cost market index because it beats most mutual funds. Only 2 out of 2,862 broad domestic stock funds were able to outperform their peers consistently over five years, according to a Dow Jones study. Wall Street takes over $560 billions from our earnings every year on the promise to provide "above average" returns. But, trading securities does NOT benefit us. pbs.org/moyers/journal/09282007/

Most wealthy people are NOT traders. They own a business that compounds their money. We can own a piece of Buffett's businesses using monthly contributions of just $250. Buffett says the real source of his success is *Compounding* and it only works if we leave our money alone and be patient.

We can be co-owners of Coke, GEICO, Fruit of the Loom, Benjamin Moore, Acme Bricks, Burlington Northern and more. By holding Buffett's BRK.B, we profit from businesses we patronize every day. We simply buy and hold stock in Buffett's holding company Berkshire Hathaway to make money over time. Investing, not speculating is all about putting our money in actual businesses that are growing so that in the future we can get our money back multiplied many times over. See page 32.

We invest in a number of successful businesses so if one fails, we still earn money every year. We want to pay few fees or taxes so that our account compounds at 20%. We want to invest a fixed amount like $250 a month (about $9 a day) automatically so we can **set it and forget it**. We check our statement only once a year. The rest of the time we DO NOTHING. Easy but hard!

As a working person, we can use a special IRS tax shelter account so we pay NO TAXES; *ever.* We can buy and hold our low-cost stocks in this special account and ALL the earnings are tax-FREE. That means we can accumulate $1 million from our $250 a month in about 23 years with Buffett. We could only do that by using a NO tax, LOW fee account. The earnings are reinvested and compounded over time for us automatically.

We avoid Wall Street's fees of 1-3% and income taxes FOREVER. Following certain simple steps, we can benefit from the FULL miracle of compounding. **We can do it ourselves in an hour and save thousands**. We don't need "professionals" because they don't know the future. We avoid their fees and keep more. Plus, all our earnings are Tax-FREE. Look at the difference:

Tax-FREE v Taxable

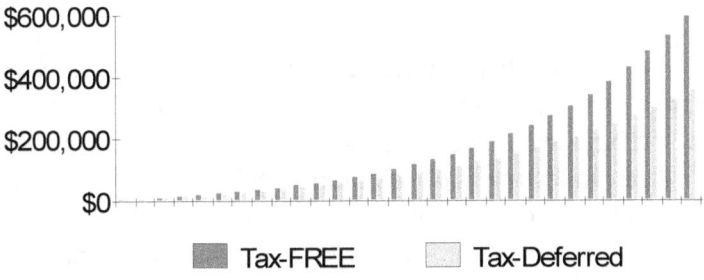

I have been in financial services for over 20 years. Wealthy people usually have their own business and reinvest their profits back in the business. Most don't know a thing about stocks but know that they can't beat the market or Mr Buffett's record.

The key factor in building wealth is TIME—letting our money make money. Mr Buffett credits the ***miracle of compounding*** for his success. We can use compounding to make money. And in a tax-FREE account we pay no taxes. Taxes and fees take away the miracle of compounding.

We don't pay taxes on the amount our account earns every year. We don't pay high fees on the balance of our account every year. Most brokers or advisors take fees no matter how much they earn or lose. We invest in a proven long-term investment—shares of growing companies—that Buffett and his partner pick.

After we accumulate a sizable balance—say $150,000—we can borrow from this account to buy things like appliances and new used cars. We avoid paying top price and interest. We also use it to cover our insurance deductibles and save by paying less premium. Of course larger risks are covered by our regular high-deductible policies. We become self-insured and self-funded like a business.

Buffett has picked investments that you can't buy through your broker. You can't copy the Buffett portfolio because some of his companies have no stock available. These investments are the kind that pension funds own at low cost.

The account you put your BRK.B shares into is a special account that uses "dollar cost averaging"—we invest the same amount monthly. It is simple to invest the same amount monthly. If you and your spouse contribute $250 a month, ***each*** of you could have $500,000 in 18-22 years. By investing a fixed amount each month, we buy shares at the least cost possible. We buy more shares when the price is low. We buy less when the price is high. Buffett buys whole companies or stocks at a discount.

If our investing is done automatically, we have a better chance of success. Automatic investing is simplicity itself. We can't miss making a contribution. The people who succeed at building wealth are those who NEVER stop investing. They use a simple plan and practice patience—just as Mr Buffett advises.

With this account, we don't need to take distributions until we want to. Most pensions and IRAs require distributions and taxes later. Heirs don't have to pay taxes on this account either.

Both of you invest in high-earning companies over time. We let the miracle of compounding work. We pay $3,000 a year over time and gain a $ million or more. We don't stop investing when the market goes up or down. We make investing automatic. The miracle happens because we do NOT SELL. We have more because we pay less! See top line on page 13.

Building wealth requires **patience**. If you are self-employed, you understand that it takes time to build a business. You have to have the right product and then find the customers to serve at a price that enables you to earn a living and a profit to expand.

If you work for others, you don't have to be a genius to become financially independent. Wealthy people control their spending by various methods. Some have goals and budgets that help them keep their spending and investing habits. Some are thrifty and don't spend more than they make. Most use CPAs not brokers.

Wealthy people have learned that there is **no quick way** to become wealthy. Mr Buffett has been at it for about 65 years. Accumulating assets requires the investing habit. They learned the habit and saw that the habit paid off over time. Their money compounds and is taxed at reduced rates.

It does not take a lot of time to manage your account. In fact, it takes only an hour to set up this account and only 1 hour a year to manage it. Building wealth is more about NOT doing something with your investments. Activity in investing is usually the result of fear or greed. Buffett says his holding period is '**forever.**' Remember Mr Potter in *__It's a Wonderful Life__*.

"Potter isn't selling. Potter's buying! And why? Because we're panicky and he's not. He's picking up some bargains."

Smart investors like Buffett buy more assets when others are selling at a loss. We can't build a small fortune overnight with a quick buy and sell strategy. **Patience** allows assets to "grow by themselves." Note on page 22 that the client's account keeps growing even after falling some years. The client never lost money because he did NOT sell in lean years!

People with assets understand that to build wealth they need to keep their money working. They do this by buying only the products they need. In fact, that has become their way of life. For instance, they can afford to buy an expensive new car but they don't because cars lose value quickly. They don't like to lose value. They invest in the businesses they own or in the securities of companies. They improve their future by buying more assets that "grow by themselves." The chart on page 32 illustrates annual stock market growth of $2,000 since 1950.

Wealthy people know about the **miracle of compounding**. Isn't it time we learn? If we invest $250 per spouse, we can have $1 million in time. $250 a month is only $9 a day. That $9 a day is building our future life. It provides more security than insurance. In a sense, having assets is the best 'lifestyle' insurance we can have.

But it is TIME—compounding—that creates wealth.

Be a Warren Buffett Millionaire

"Our favorite holding period is forever."

"You don't need to be a rocket scientist."

"To invest successfully, you need not understand beta, efficient markets, modern portfolio theory, option pricing or emerging markets.
You may, in fact, be better off knowing nothing of these.

"Over the long term, the stock market news will be good. Despite two World Wars, depressions, the Dow rose from 66 to 11,497."

"We will continue to ignore political and economic forecasts."

"Our investments continue to be few in number and simple in concept."

Warren Buffett

1

Buy and hold just one stock

Building a $1 million asset takes time. If we own a business, it might take a lifetime. We would have to find and sell the right product to the right customer in a profitable manner. It is difficult to come up with a completely new product or way to sell it like Apple has done. If we are lucky, we could buyout our boss after working at a skilled trade for years. Many wealthy people have followed this path.

Building a **Wealth** account must begin where we are. To build wealth is to take some of our salary from working for others and buy certain stocks of growing companies. We can each accumulate $500,000 over time. If we both buy Buffett's stock in tax-FREE account, it will take less time.

We can see how this can happen by checking the growth of the broad market index fund shown on page 32. **Time is the key** to building wealth. Wealthy people typically invest in many types of investments, businesses and real estate. We begin with one stock we buy every month for $250. That one stock BRK.A or BRK.B owns many businesses.

If we are going to accumulate $500,000 each, we need to be patient. Buffett may not earn 20.8% each year. The market earns 10% to 12% a year, on average, over time. We must understand the reward and risk tradeoff. If we want to have a $1 million in the future, we could wait 80 years for our $500 a month to grow in a bank at 2% or wait about 20 years in his company stocks. We are using TIME instead of the bank's guarantee to pay interest **every day**. We don't need that guarantee. We need the high probability that Buffett's companies will grow over time. Buffett has proved his skills over the long-term: 20% for 50 years.

Investing in stocks provides our best chance of success. The value of a stock market index—a bunch of stocks—has varied greatly in any one year. However, over any 10 years, the value has

ALWAYS increased. This is the reason wealthy people have most of their money in the stocks of growing companies.

Remember, we are looking for investments that compound our money **over time**. The reward profile of owning a bunch of stocks is like owning a growing business—in any one year, we might have a loss or a gain. But over time we have more profits than losses and thus accumulate $1,000,000.

Range of annual returns of stocks, 1950 – 2000

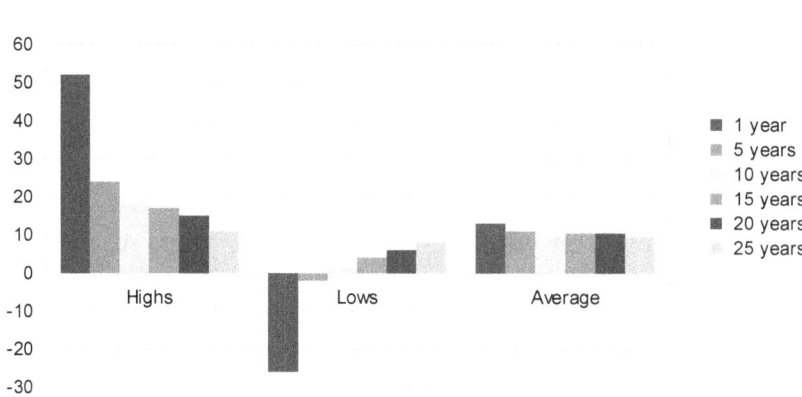

Buffett's BRK.B has had 2 bad years in 50 years. Bank savings are subject to long-term inflation but are a great place to park our money for a year in case we need it to repair our car, appliances or house. However, bank savings are not really an investment. People who put their money in the bank because they think it is "safe" are not thinking about the long-term. Bank accounts are actually *losing* money. Inflation is eating away at the value of their savings.

Inflation is about 3% historically. If we earn 3% or less on our money, we are losing purchasing power. This means that it now costs $0.49 to mail a first class letter instead of $0.06 as it did in 1970. The cost of sending a letter went up at about 5% a year. In order to have enough money to buy anything in retirement, we are going to need to invest our LONG-TERM money in an investment earning more than 5%. This goes for all the money we will need to buy things in the future.

There are few investments that we can buy that have the same long-term annual returns of stocks of growing companies. The graph below presents the relative growth of different types of investments and inflation. Over long-periods of time, government bonds grow at a rate a little above the rate of inflation. Large company stocks like GE and P&G grow at a higher rate and thus accumulate larger values in our account. Smaller companies grow much faster and make our account even larger over time. However, as the graph shows, the index line can be very jagged on a monthly and even yearly basis. Values do go up over time.

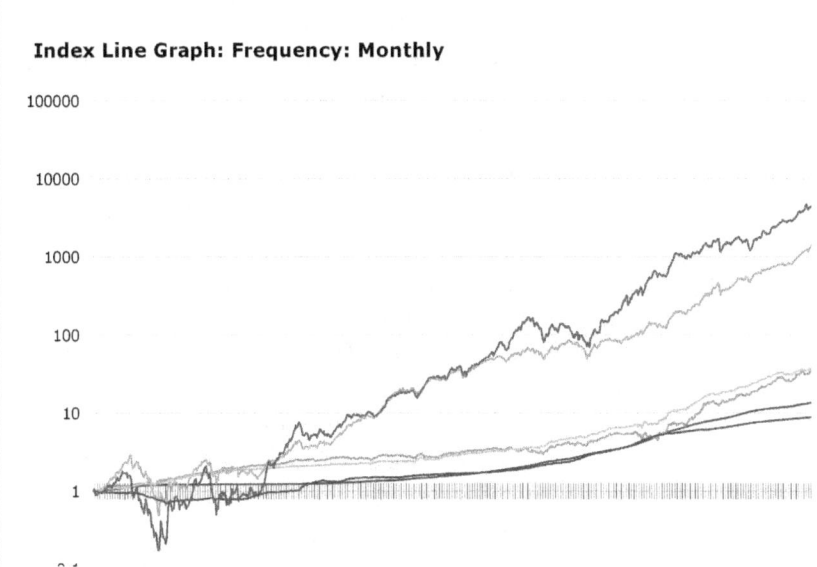

Index Line Graph: Frequency: Monthly

Top line—Small Cap Stocks
2nd line—Large Cap Stocks (S&P 500)
3rd line—US Long-term Corporate Bonds
4th line—Intermediate-term Government Bonds
5th line—US 30 day Government T-bills
6th line—US inflation

Courtesy: Dr. Campbell R. Harvey http://www.duke.edu/~charvey/

This graph makes it pretty clear that in order to accumulate $1,000,000 from monthly contributions, we must buy and hold the securities of growing companies worldwide, at cost, AND pay **zero** tax on the growth to maximize compounding. We can see clearly that investing in growing company stocks is more likely to get us to our goal in our lifetime than investing in government bonds or a bank savings account. **Investing requires the long view**.

This graph shows the accumulation over time without paying taxes each year on our earnings or annual fees to an advisor or broker. It does show that over most periods greater than 10 years, our account value grows more with stocks.

Some wealthy people also invest in gold, real estate, and alternative investment schemes. But these investments do NOT usually represent a large portion of their portfolio. These investments do not come without significant costs and significant risk. They do NOT show the same consistent long-term growth pattern that growing global companies do.

According to a number of studies, gold, real estate and other investments have annual average returns under 10%. When we subtract the costs of buying, maintaining and securing these other investments, we give up a lot of the gains. We can use an online compounding calculator to become familiar with total accumulations at different rates of return—3, 5, 7, 9, 11, 18, etc. http://www.moneychimp.com/calculator/compound_interest_calculator.htm

For instance, if an investment requires taxes to be paid each year, this cancels some of the compounding effect on the total accumulation over time. Since we wish to reach $1 million as soon as possible, we must use a tax-FREE account to hold our low-cost investments. Depending on our tax bracket (taxable income) we may reduce our total accumulation by over half because we lose the compounding effect. The chart below gives us an idea of what can happen in 30 years. Most retirement accounts are tax-DEFERRED; not tax-FREE. Taxes have to be paid sometime.

As you have probably guessed, the wealthy have already figured out how to pay less tax on their wealth. The American tax system taxes earned income at higher rates than investment income. Plus we must pay federal and state income taxes, excise taxes, Social Security and Medicare taxes, perhaps unemployment and disability income taxes as well as sales tax on most goods.

For the wealthy, like Warren Buffett, with $ billions of assets, most of his income is from his company stock gains and dividends. He admitted, "I pay at a lower overall tax rate than all of my office employees." He pays only 17% **total** tax versus 33%. Listen and weep: http://www.youtube.com/watch?v=Cu5B-2LoC4s.

We are not wealthy yet. Most of us have income which is taxed as earned income and goes straight to the government before we have a chance to pay less tax. Even self-employed people must pay taxes as they go—at least once a quarter. Only the wealthy and large companies can afford most tax avoidance schemes. Fortunately, Congress created one for working people. The Roth IRA lets us avoid income tax on the earnings altogether.

Tax-FREE v Taxable

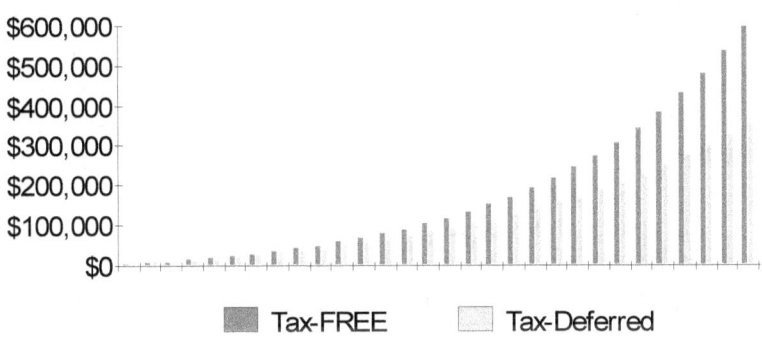

In order for us to become wealthy we must find a way to avoid paying tax on our $1,000,000 accounts as they accumulate. Traditional pensions, 401k and IRAs just delay taxes—taxes must be paid later as the money comes out of the account AND at higher earned income tax rates. Thus even when our investment money is growing it is converted to earned income money for tax purposes. Unlike Mr Buffett, we NEVER get to pay the wealthy people (capital gains) rate of 15-20%.

Now we have a solution: 0% tax. We use the Roth IRA, a tax-FREE trust, to compound the high returns of the stocks of growing companies over time. We avoid the greatest killer of wealth—taxes —and let time transform our contributions into $ millions. Patience and simple buy and hold investing in a tax-FREE account make our strategy beat the industry's "professional" stock pickers.

The hard part of investing is leaving our money alone to work for you. Remember, you are building a business not playing roulette.

In order to buy stock in Buffett's holding company, Berkshire Hathaway, we must buy shares from a broker. We don't need a full service broker since we are only buying BRK'B as a "market order." That means our $250 will buy partial shares at the price on the exchange at the time our broker decides.

Some brokerage firms use dollar-cost averaging as their simple stock buying mechanism. For instance, to reduce costs, our broker will collect all the orders for a stock during the week and buy the total of them on Tuesday. Capital One offers the ShareBuilder Plan which offers us a method of investing a fixed amount each month at the low cost of $3.95 per transaction.
https://www.capitaloneinvesting.com/main/pricing-trading.aspx

This compares with other brokers who charge $6.95 to 19.95. There is no monthly fee to maintain the account nor a minimum to begin buying. Capital One will reinvest your dividends in the stock for free so you can compound your earnings. Be sure to read the reviews like this one: https://www.nerdwallet.com/blog/investing/sharebuilder-capital-one-investing-review/

Compare other brokerage firms for their monthly investing plans. There are many plans and charge/fee schedules so read the fine print before you invest. If you set up a monthly fixed amount buying plan, make sure the broker can buy partial shares and reinvest your dividends automatically. Read what other brokers offer at http://www.broker-reviews.us/.

We want a low-cost investing plan:
Account type: Roth IRA
Minimum: $0
Trades: Market order $3.95 partial shares
Reinvest dividends: $0
Automatic bank account debit for dollar-cost averaging
Quarterly statement and tax documentation free

Join the Warren Buffett millionaire club!

2

Your tax-favored investment account

The solution to our problem came in 1997. Senator Roth (DE) introduced the Roth IRA. This tax-FREE account provides the protection we need to allow our contributions to compound without taxation every year AND later when we take them out, we never have to pay taxes on the earnings, dividends and interest we earn on our money. We don't even pay the tax-advantaged rate the wealthy pay! We pay 0% not 20%; not 33%.

Ben Franklin was wrong! Only death is certain, not taxes. The only thing we give up with this account is an immediate tax deduction. However, compare the value of paying a little more tax (15%-25% on $3,000) now with paying ZERO tax later. We can spend $30,000 tax-FREE for every $3,000 a year we contributed over time. We can see the fantastic advantage we now have. This is a better deal than most wealthy people have.

Tax-FREE accumulation and tax-FREE income after age 59.5 is a huge bonus. It is like receiving $300,000 FREE on our $1 million accounts. Also, because we already paid tax on the contributions, we pay no tax when we take this money out for emergencies. This can make a big impact on our borrowing costs when we take money out to buy appliances, used cars, a home down payment or living expenses.

Using this account, both our total contributions over time grow to over $1,000,000 and we don't have to pay any federal or state income tax on the earnings. WOW! Since we pay no tax, Uncle Sam is really helping us out in meeting our goals. All we have to do is use this special IRS tax shelter and keep making contributions. We **Keep More of What We Earn**.

This special account is the IRS §408 trust. We have to follow the rules to gain this amazing tax advantage but the Roth IRA rules are pretty simple—taxed money goes in and tax-FREE earnings come out after age 59 ½. We can take our contributions out anytime.

Why is this account special? Every other type of investment account requires that taxes be paid now or later. Mutual funds declare gains each year just like a bank CD and we need to pay tax. Our retirement accounts and annuities are tax-deferred not FREE. We pay tax when we take money out. Even life insurance with cash value requires taxes to be paid unless it is a death benefit to heirs. Even assets like individual stocks or ETFs or our own company equity held for long term gains will require taxes eventually when sold. The gains in this account are FREE—no tax ever.

Contributions are limited to $5,500 (2016), but may rise in future years. https://www.irs.gov/pub/irs-pdf/p590a.pdf There are income limits of $132,000 (2016) or $194,000 married. We make our checking debit to our Roth IRA **accounts** automatic so our broker buys the stock each month automatically.

We may also invest in our employer's Roth 401k if it is offered. The contributions grow tax-FREE forever. We can contribute more to this account. We will have tax-FREE income from the account later. Contributions to a regular 401k can be converted later. We can limit taxes by converting small portions of our 401k or regular IRA each year.

We can make contributions to our Roth 401k if our employer offers it in the retirement plan. We may prefer to be taxed *before* our retirement since tax rates are bound to be higher later and our balances are smaller at the beginning.

There are no limits on an employee's income in determining if he or she can make designated Roth 401(k) contributions. If we decide to invest $3,000 a year for about 23 years in Buffett's stock or a stock fund inside our employer's Roth 401k plan, we could accumulate $1 million with NO income taxation on the earnings. The tax savings might be worth an extra 30% since our federal and state taxes are avoided. We **Keep More of What We Earn**.

The catch: If we take the *earnings* out before age 59.5, we must pay income tax, unless we use $10,000 for our first home, are disabled, or die. The account must be open at least 5 years to take money out. However, if we take out contributions, *we pay no tax*. If we pay our 'loan' back to our own account, we can still reach our goal. The hard part is leaving our money alone to grow tax-FREE.

Let's say we need $25,000 to buy a used luxury car. As we can see from the chart on page 22, taking $25,000 from an account worth $250,000 is very different from taking $25,000 from one worth only $45,000. Both may be contributions (not taxable) but borrowing 60% of the account this early stunts its growth.

A patient millionaire finds a way to save the $25,000 separately or keep driving the old car. The power of compounding is too valuable to lose by raiding the account too early. One story about billionaire Buffett will illustrate the habits of the wealthy. Mr Buffett is said to have driven (no chauffeur) his VW Beetle long after he became a multi-billionaire. Buffett did not like to lose money and a new car loses 40% of its value quickly. He thought that the $40,000-new-car cost, invested at 20%, is worth about $80,000 in 4 years. So he kept driving the old VW.

Most clients are not that thrifty. They use their contributions to buy a used car to avoid new car depreciation and new appliances, vacations, and other necessities AFTER they have a sizable account. When both family wage earners contribute to their Roth IRAs, they can easily reach a half million dollars in 15 years. That means $90,000 are contributions and then some of it can be used to pay cash instead of buying on credit.

Wealthy people use their wealth to pay cash. They never PAY interest except in business. Paying interest on a debt is the reverse of compounding. Someone else is becoming wealthy from us. The wealthy always EARN interest. They use the calculator at http://www.moneychimp.com/calculator/compound_interest_calculator.htm to determine what the real cost of buying something on credit will be just like Buffett did. Why give up $80,000 when we can drive the old car a little longer. Buffett could have bought 100 new cars and it wouldn't have changed his wealth or lifestyle, but he didn't. His habit is to live frugally and not look wealthy.

We can use this account (its contributions) to cover our liability insurance deductibles also. We can save thousands of dollars by using the highest deductibles on our car, home and health insurance. Self-insurance is also the way to avoid any changes in our policy costs. Insurers are less likely to drop us if we don't make claims for small amounts. If we take care of our out-of-pocket medical expenses, we may find a low-cost comprehensive policy if we need to buy health coverage.

The rules for the use of our Roth IRA account are manageable by ourselves. We don't need an advisor. They are found at irs.gov/retirement/article/0,,id=137307,00.html. Our account trustee can answer most questions. We don't need to pay an attorney. All of the large low-cost brokers and mutual fund firms are trustees. We will discuss the best firms available below.

We can start this account with any of the firms with no upfront charges. Most do charge an annual fee for the investments and an annual bookkeeping fee. We will consider the specific investment options later. We will use low-cost firms only—we keep more.

It is important to pick a trustee with the least costs since over time the annual costs can really destroy our accumulations. For instance, if we use a regular broker as trustee, we might have to pay 2-3% each year on the balance—reducing our totals by up to 63%. If both spouses have a low-cost account with contributions of $250 a month for about 22 years, they could both accumulate $1,000,000. If they use a broker/advisor, both accounts may hit only $500,000. Depending on the earnings, using a broker/advisor (fees of 2-3% per year), they could really hurt themselves. We need to avoid high costs. We compare the benefits of firms below.

We can open our Roth IRA account at any age as long as we have *earned* income. Any job will do. We don't even need a job requiring a W-2 to prove it. A part-time, weekend or night job will do. Any cash-only work will also qualify. Accountants recommend that receipts and records be maintained. We could even work for ourselves in a home-office business. A business also provides tax advantages in retirement.

Nontaxable distributions from a Roth IRA won't affect our eligibility for a child's student aid. Later, in retirement, this money won't raise the taxes on our Social Security benefits.

We can make contributions to both our individual Roth IRA and our Roth account at work (Roth401k). The limits change each year, so check: https://www.irs.gov/pub/irs-prior/p590a--2014.pdf

Avoiding taxes on the annual gains of our accumulations is one of the few Congressional tax havens for working people. This special account is the IRS §408 trust. We have to follow the rules of a Roth IRA to gain this amazing tax advantage. The rules are pretty simple: pay smaller tax on contributions now in exchange for NO tax on huge gains later—over time, $66,000 is taxed so $934,000 is *never taxed*. We can use the contributions to avoid paying interest to banks for our major purchases. **We earn interest, we don't pay interest**. This account is the perfect tax shelter for working people. And it is simple to set up and run each year with our Buffett stock tax-FREE account.

In the future, we can spend $45,000 tax-FREE for every $3,000 we invested with Buffett each year.

Join the Warren Buffett millionaire club!

Actual client, Tom's account, investing $3,000 per year, 1962-2003

24%	3,720
16%	7,795
12%	12,091
-10%	13,582
24%	20,561
11%	26,153
-8%	26,821
4%	31,013
14%	38,775
19%	49,713
-14%	45,333
-26%	35,766
37%	53,110
24%	69,576
-8%	66,770
6%	73,956
18%	90,809
32%	123,827
-5%	120,486
22%	150,653
21%	185,920
6%	200,255
32%	268,297
19%	322,843
5%	342,135
17%	403,808
32%	536,987
-3%	523,787
31%	690,091
8%	748,538
10%	826,692
2%	846,286
38%	1,172,015
23%	1,445,268
33%	1,926,197
28%	2,469,372
21%	2,991,570
-9%	2,725,059
-12%	2,403,420
-22%	1,874,601
29%	2,412,905

3

Compound high earnings: Buffett's 20.8%

Compounding high earnings is key. The rich get richer—the top 1% take 23.5% of all income (up from 8.9%). And, as many millionaires have said, "the first million is the hardest." If we start with $250 a month, it will take us about 22 years of investing in Buffett stock to reach $1,000,000. (And only in a tax-FREE low-fee account.) However, when we reach **1** million dollars, we only have to double our money to reach $2 million. Investors in his stock, earning 20% on average, do this in about 5 years without adding new money. Our low-fee tax-FREE account makes it easier to reach our goal. We pay no advisor costs because we use a simple strategy and let the Berkshire Hathaway businesses make us rich.

Compounding of high earnings means that we make money on our last period's accumulations. The progression looks like the client's account values on the previous page. Notice that our balance can double in a few good years. This happens because we are not just adding money each month, but adding up to 38% of the previous year's accumulation to our balance. We are making money on previous earnings with no extra effort on our part. During this 40 year period, this client 'lost' money some years. In fact, he lost 14% and then 26% back to back, but then made 37% and 24%.

Wealthy people don't panic and sell. They have learned that compounding over the long term is the only way they can build wealth. Get-rich-quick schemes only benefit the operators. To reach their goal, the rich know there will be setbacks. No business grows steadily upward all the time. They have seen the losses before and know their values will return. They remain **patient**.

We will buy assets that "grow by themselves." We will have security because our ***purchasing power*** will grow over time. If we doubt that the wealthy invest in the stock market for security, take a look at the long-term returns for various Vanguard mutual funds where they put their money. These funds have provided investors with $1,000,000 or more for their retirement. During the recent recession, Vanguard had inflows not outflows.

The wealthy earn 10% to 12% on their money from the market. We could buy *Vanguard's Top Ten* and receive over 10% total return with less risk than owning just one stock or fund. When one stock or fund is down, others are up. We own them all.

2014 Total Return	Fund	Long-term Return	Longevity
13.5%	500 Index	11.1%*	since 1976
-14.3%	Energy	11.5%	since 1984
7.4%	Extended Market Idx	11.1%	since 1987
28.5%	Health	17.4%	since 1984
-5.6%	International Growth	10.6%	since 1981
18.7%	PRIMECAP	13.9%	since 1984
7.5%	Small Cap Index	9.3%	since 1960
8.1%	Wellesley Income	10.1%	since 1970
11.8%	Windsor	11.6%	since 1958
11.2%	Windsor II	11.1%	since 1985
8.7%	Average	11.8%	

*Average Annual Returns as of 12/31/14.

However, Warren Buffett has found the BEST firms so he earns 20.8% for us over time. This kind of security comes from his simple strategy of <u>patience</u>. The *miracle of compounding* works its magic on our money when we give it TIME. The wealthy give their money time to compound. They don't try to time the market with buys and sells. They avoid tax on gains this way. They maintain their contribution schedule because each $3,000 added is worth $45,000 to them later. They use the compound interest calculator so they know the future value:
<u>moneychimp.com/calculator/compound_interest_calculator.htm</u>.

Compounding of high earnings requires patience but has a big bang. Most people who become wealthy have learned the blessings of waiting. At the beginning of the accumulation, especially if we have a loss or two, we may get discouraged and quit. The account just doesn't seem to adding up to an inspiring total.

It took this client 21 years to get to $150,000. Then it only took 14 years to get to a $1,172,015. After only 4 years, it became

$3,000,000. Shortly thereafter he "lost" over a million dollars!

This client stuck with it and is now successful in completing his goal but there are many who have not. Most people who are not wealthy already, have a hard time believing it can happen with their *patience*. They just don't have the experience of how compounding works to keep faith in its outcome eventually.

If you already have a Roth IRA with significant values, you can use it to do your gift and estate planning. You don't have to take the money out beginning at age 70½, unlike the regular IRA or pension. You can let it grow. You can name your family members as beneficiaries which will extend the miracle of compounding. Obviously, as beneficiary, your grandchild could just liquidate the account and thus lose the value of their "Gift of a Lifetime." Wealthy people use a knowledgable attorney to make sure their wealth passes to those who will make the most of it.

Once an account becomes sizable, we don't need to add contributions to it. Usually, by the time we stop regular employment, we aren't making contributions. This account cannot accept contributions unless they are the result of *earned* income. Some wealthy people continue to work after age 65 because they love what they do and want to continue. Obviously, they don't need to work. The **miracle of compounding continues** all their lives.

One of the best examples of the potential of growth by compounding is seen in the accumulation of investor Anne Scheiber. With below average wages, this woman invested in quality companies which paid dividends and gains. There were no Roth IRAs then. She reinvested her dividends and gains and at her death *gave $22 million* to Yeshiva University for a scholarship designed to help support women.

Earl Crawley, parking lot attendant, is another example: http://www.youtube.com/watch?v=XD0svDGyLWU Getting "the first half million is the hardest." Since we don't make millions, compounding high earnings is the only way we are going to reach our goal in our lifetime. Compounding works because we leverage TIME and high earnings on high earnings. We *Keep More of What We Earn* with low-fee tax-FREE accounts.

Only patience allows our accumulations to compound.

The annual returns of growing companies

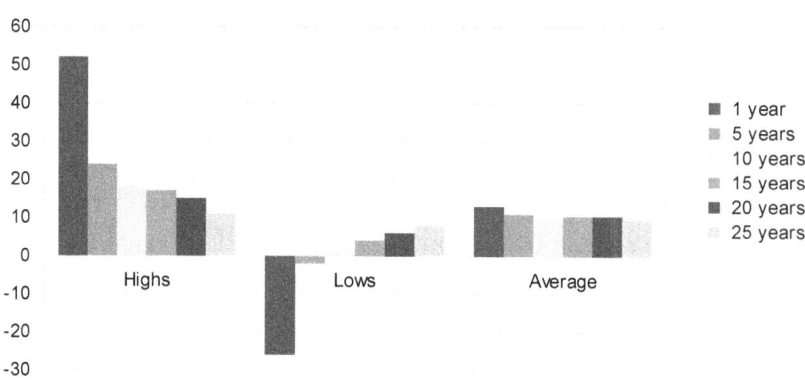

Range of annual returns of stocks, 1950 – 2000

4

Automate contributions

Our simple strategy for building wealth requires consistent additions to our accounts. Making it automatic helps take our emotions out of the process. **We gain true power.** We do not panic like others. We do not watch the market or our account. If we don't have to write and send the contribution check each month, we won't think about how the market or our account is doing.

Our normal reaction to having money in an account is to watch it, guard it, think about how it is doing, compare its size and rate of growth. We pay advisors to watch too. All of these actions are not good for a business. Remember, we are silent partners in growing companies. We have to believe that global businesses will continue to grow. However, most people don't look at their wealth-building in that way. Most people do not think of their accounts as a stake in many growing businesses. They consider them to be casinos.

One way we can help change our thinking is to try to put the account out of our immediate concern by making the contributions automatic. Like the Social Security contributions we make every payday, the contributions are made automatically. This can happen easily with a Roth 401k since our Plan will deduct the amount we specify at Plan enrollment. In the same manner, we can have the Roth IRA trustee debit our checking account automatically every month until we cancel.

As one client told me, "I never see the deduction, so I never miss it." Of course this client had already identified the $250 he had committed to his $2,000,000 future years ago. He says that he would just waste the $250 on a car lease anyway. He had been doing that for years because he never took the trouble to set his goals for short-term and long-term timelines. Then he went through his spending with a knife. He used our Guides to find the $250 a month he was wasting on products and services he would never use or need. In Dan Keppel's amazon.com/Insiders-Guides-Discount-Financial-Services/ you will find "tricks of the trade" that we insiders use to buy directly from quality manufacturers.

Many people have trouble keeping up the habit of investing every month. Some emergency always interupts this process. The delay in the periodic contributions causes the compounding effect to be reduced. The interruption is like starting the investment process late. This chart shows us what starting early or not putting off the investments can do. Over time, the delay compounds the lack of accumulation. Starting 5 years later means ending up with HALF the amount we were shooting for. It is hard to believe that missing that $250 a month for 5 years or $15,000 can reduce our total from $600,000 to $300,000. It's easy to say **I will start later**.

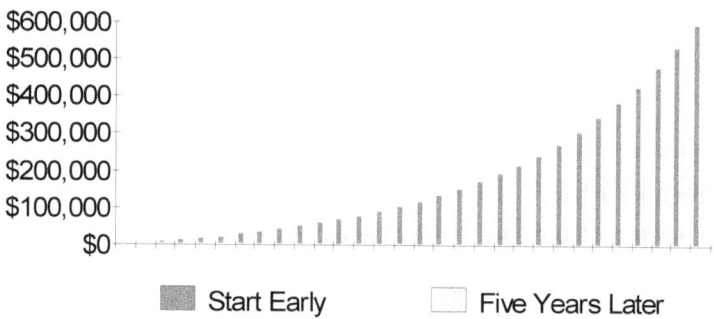

The Value of Starting Early

And we can't make it up by adding $15,000 later.

This is why our contributions need to be automatic: Don't rely on writing a check each month. We should have the money taken directly from our bank account by the trustee. Contributions are after-tax so we can take them for any emergency. Nontaxable distributions from a Roth IRA won't affect your eligibility for your student's school aid either. Later, in retirement, this money won't affect your Social Security benefits, which are subject to taxation depending on your income. Even tax-free municipal bond income is counted in the tax worksheet for Social Security benefits.
irs.gov/pub/irs-pdf/p915.pdf

The second reason why this technique for developing wealth works is that when contributions are automatic, we do not have the temptation to try to time the market. Many people want to know the secret to timing the market so that they can invest at the bottom of market cycles and sell at the peak of the market.

Unfortunately, it is a myth that anyone can do this over time. Again, this is a misconception of how building wealth works. Yes, there are lucky gamblers. However, they are the exception. We use Buffett's **Wealth** strategy: patience. We want to end up with $1,000,000 tax-FREE. We are silent partners in businesses that produce dividends and gains over time. We are NOT placing our contributions on the red or black at the casino. Look at page 22.

Our account grows with steady contributions because in the month we buy shares in <u>BRK.B</u> or a stock mutual fund, we receive fewer shares when the price is high and more shares when the price is low. Studies have shown that this is better than investing our $3,000/$6,000 all at once. It is not possible to know when the shares we buy will be at their lowest cost in the year going forward. Again, over time, we will own more shares at the least cost because we are buying more when the price is low and less when high.

This can be illustrated by considering how hard it is to find the lowest price at any given time in the market. There were ONLY <u>40 days</u> from 1950 to 2007 that produced 70% of all the S&P 500 index's total returns. That is <u>40 out of 14,528</u>. We can't possibly know when to buy into the businesses represented in the mutual fund we are using. We will lose money if we become traders who try to time the market well. Traders lose money most of the time. See John Bogle's analysis in *Don't Count on It*, p 169.

The key to accumulating **Wealth** is patience not gambling: let compounding work. Over time, stocks of growing companies have the most consistent record of providing 10%-12% annual returns. We just don't know which companies and which time to invest are best. Luckily, we don't have to know. We just need to understand compounding and keep buying high return stocks or funds.

The bigger picture is that we want our account accumulation to grow exponentially. We want to take advantage of the miracle of compounding. Since we don't have wealth now, we are going to have to be patient to acquire it. We want every dollar we invest to count. We have $250/$500 a month to invest so we have to rely on consistent buying of shares to reach our goal.

Accumulations double in value every 8-10 years if they are concentrated in the top two lines below. Of course the stock market doesn't move up at 10-12% EACH year. However, our account will double and double and double so that in about 26 years, we could have $1/2 million each. Notice how the account values in the chart on page 22 for this client double—from $1 million to $2 million in 8 years, even with 3 years of losses. Of course, a million dollars will be worth less in the future because of inflation. But we will certainly appreciate our account values later no matter what our contributions are now. Consistency over time builds wealth.

Cumulative Wealth

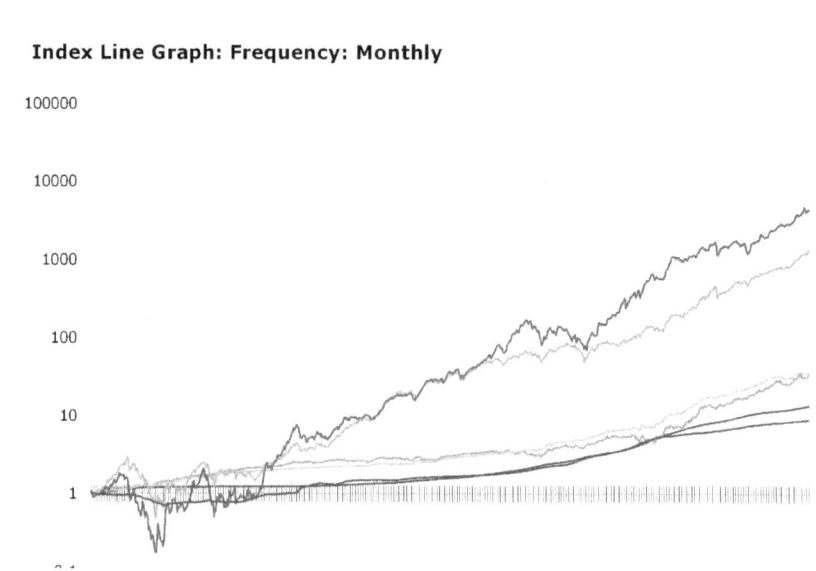

Top line—Small Cap Stocks
2nd line—Large Cap Stocks (S&P 500)
3rd line—US Long-term Corporate Bonds
4th line—Intermediate-term Government Bonds
5th line—US 30 day Government T-bills
6th line—US inflation

Courtesy: Dr. Campbell R. Harvey http://www.duke.edu/~charvey/

And the bonus of this geometric account growth is that it does not quit even after we stop adding our monthly contributions. Once the account has reached a certain mass, let's say after 20 years of $6K contributions or $120,000, it will keep compounding. On page 32 we show you how this worked for contributions of $2,000 to a virtual account invested in the U.S. stock market (top 500 firms) over time.

We see in the chart "**Cumulative Wealth**" above that wealth accumulates at different rates depending on the type of assets we buy. For anyone who invested in smaller companies over any given 15 year period, the benefits were outstanding. For each $1,000 invested in 1940, $3,000,000 was the total return by the 1990's. Investing more cautiously in the large companies of the S&P 500, for instance, our $1,000 would have grown to almost a $1,000,00 by 2000. Yes, the lines are not perfectly straight, but growing $500 a month to $1,000,000 is definitely worth the ups and downs. Inflation is designated by the bottom line here. Putting all our money in the bank for 'safety' would accumulate at a rate represented by a line near that bottom line.

Warren Buffett has earned 20.8% a year on average so we can expect our accumulations may be faster. However, there is no guarantee. That said, Buffett has 50 years of experience at winning.

Of course, these different rates of wealth accumulation assume two important factors—NO taxes and LOW costs. We have eliminated the first killer of wealth—TAXES—by using a tax-FREE trust account. Costs of the investment type we use can also kill your total accumulations. The whole financial industry is built on the extraction of these costs from the accounts of investors. We must use low-cost stock funds to have a *Tax-FREE Retirement*.

One of the most difficult parts of creating **Wealth** is sticking with the program. If we put our monthly contributions on automatic, we will succeed. If we instruct our trustee to debit our savings or checking account every month, we have a high probability of meeting our goals over time. We set it and forget it.

We forget we are investing in our future and thus we actually create one. What an irony!

Year	Returns	Balance	Balance	Balance	Balance
		$2,000			
1950	31%	$2,620			
1951	24%	$5,729			
1952	18%	$9,120			
1953	-1%	$11,009			
1954	52%	$19,773			
1955	31%	$28,523			
1956	5%	$32,049			
1957	-11%	$30,304			
1958	43%	$46,194			
1959	12%	$53,978			
1960	1%	$56,538			
1961	26%	$73,757			
1962	-8%	$69,697			
1963	24%	$88,904			
1964	16%	$105,449			
1965	12%	$120,342			
1966	-10%	$110,108			
1967	24%	$139,014			
1968	11%	$156,526			
1969	-8%	$145,844	2,000		
1970	4%	$153,757	2,080		
1971	14%	$177,563	4,651		
1972	19%	$213,681	7,915		
1973	-14%	$185,485	8,527		
1974	-26%	$138,739	7,790		
1975	37%	$192,813	13,412		
1976	24%	$241,568	19,111		
1977	-8%	$224,082	19,422		
1978	6%	$239,647	22,707		
1979	18%	$285,144	29,155	2,000	
1980	32%	$379,030	41,124	2,640	
1981	-5%	$361,978	40,968	4,408	
1982	22%	$444,053	52,421	7,818	
1983	21%	$539,724	65,850	11,879	
1984	6%	$574,228	71,921	14,712	
1985	32%	$760,621	97,575	22,060	
1986	19%	$907,519	118,494	28,632	
1987	5%	$954,995	126,519	32,163	
1988	17%	$1,119,684	150,367	39,971	
1989	32%	$1,480,623	201,125	55,402	2,000
1990	-3%	$1,438,144	197,031	55,680	1,940
1991	31%	$1,886,589	260,731	75,560	5,161
1992	8%	$2,039,676	283,749	83,765	7,734
1993	10%	$2,245,843	314,324	94,342	10,708
1994	2%	$2,292,800	322,651	98,268	12,962
1995	38%	$3,166,824	448,018	138,370	20,647
1996	23%	$3,897,654	553,522	172,656	27,856
1997	33%	$5,186,540	738,844	232,292	39,709
1998	28%	$6,641,331	948,281	299,894	53,387
1999	21%	$8,038,430	1,149,839	365,291	67,019
2000	-9%	$7,316,791	1,048,174	334,235	62,807
2001	-12%	$6,447,855	925,203	296,223	57,095
2002	-22%	$5,024,437	722,291	232,316	46,035
2003	29%	$6,459,474	930,787	301,119	61,730
2004	11%	$7,164,483	1,034,274	336,099	70,664
2005	5%	$7,512,677	1,084,540	352,433	74,098
2006	15%	$8,694,884	1,259,259	412,409	90,450
2007	5%	$9,163,538	1,327,133	434,638	95,325
2008	-39%	$5,601,431	813,388	268,074	60,754
2009	27%	$7,116,358	952,155	342,993	79,699
2010	15%	$8,186,112	1,097,278	396,742	93,954
2011	2%	$8,347,378	1,118,894	404,558	95,805
2012	16%	$9,666,264	1,295,679	468,478	110,942
2013	32%	$12,759,468	1,710,296	618,390	146,443
Avg.	12%	12%	11%	13%	11%

Ibbotson Associates **Stocks average 11.4% per year, bonds 5%, CDs 3%.** Stocks have gone up as much as 54% and as low as –43% in 1 year, up to 28% or down to –12% in 5 years, up 20% or down 0% in 10 years, up 18% or up 3% in 20 years. Short term bonds have gone up 14% or up 0% in 1 year, up 11% or up 0% in 5 years, up 9% or up 0% in 10 years, up 10% or up 1% in 20 years. Check: returns: http://www.moneychimp.com/features/market_cagr.htm

32

5

Use a **low-cost** broker or funds

**"In every single time period and data point tested,
low-cost funds beat high-cost funds."**

Wall Street claims that you must pay more for good returns. Some pay a lot to those who predict. But fund-rating analysts at Morningstar proved that ***Wall Street is wrong***. Low-cost funds always beat high-cost funds. Lao Tzu was right: predictors don't have knowledge. No one can predict the future.

The **best predictor** of your wealth-building success is COST. It is common sense that there are just too many variables in the success of growing companies' stocks for anyone to be able to pick them in advance, consistently. The exception is Buffett. He buys only when there is clear "margin of safety." In the same way, low-cost mutual funds provide the best chance of maximizing our accumulations over time. Even Buffett can't know the future.

Despite Buffett's proven success, Wall Street continues its B..S.. that its high-paid managers know which stocks will rise. Other than BRK, if our account holds a broad representation of stocks and our investment costs are low, we will benefit over the long haul. We own the market average of 10-12% and that is better than the average Wall Street account return of 3.79%.

If we don't like putting all our money in one stock, BRK.A or B, we want to pick the lowest cost mutual fund available. A stock fund that reflects an overall market is called an index fund. This kind of fund, explained below, costs only 0.05% ($5 per $10,000). Our account will compound at or near the 10-12% over time since our fund costs 98% less than Wall Street's picks. If we use the high-cost stock funds, we will earn only 7-9% over time. These funds pay managers high salaries with expensive bonuses. The fund owners and sales staff are also paid well.

The chart below makes it clear. Over time, the costs we pay

each year will cut our total accumulation by a 50-60%. Instead of compounding at 10-12% annually on average, some people give up 1-3% of the earnings on their money to the middle person.

Cost Matters: 0.19% v 1.68%

Wall Street says that we can earn more by paying a star manager to pick the right stocks on an ongoing basis. The money "experts" say we get what we pay for and a proven stock-picking manager will overcome the extra costs and make more for us.

The reality is that this **myth has been proven wrong**. The lowest cost funds don't pay a star manager and owner big bucks but come out ahead over time. There are simply too many variables for anyone or computer program to pick the winning stocks all the time. Some of the lowest cost funds are called index funds. When we buy a market index, we are buying a piece of many companies. This gives us the same annual returns as the overall market over time. We pay tiny expenses. *We keep more*!

Many studies have proven that index funds beat funds run by stock pickers most of the time. Low-cost index funds beat 86% of funds with a stock-picking manager. *BusinessWeek* Apr 2009. http://www.businessweek.com/investing/insights/blog/archives/200 9/04/where_have_all.html.

When we investigate the experiences of the best unbiased money managers in the world, we find they recommend index funds to most people who invest as silent partners. Here are their statements:

Warren Buffett is probably history's greatest investor, in terms of results with $67 BILLION ($67 thousand million dollars) so far.

He buys and HOLDS *companies* that provide valuable products/
services to a great number of people. His company owns parts of
Coke, GEICO, Fruit of the Loom, Benjamin Moore, Acme Bricks,
Burlington Northern, etc. berkshirehathaway.com/

He told Reuters: "A very low-cost index is going to beat a
majority of the amateur-managed money or professionally-
managed money."

A fund's chance of beating the market in EACH year is 3 out of
100. nytimes.com/2009/02/22/your-money/stocks-and-bonds/22stra.html
Current winners will be next year's losers. nytimes.com/2014/07/27/
your-money/heads-or-tails-either-way-you-might-beat-a-stock-picker.html

Peter Lynch, brilliant manager, Magellan Fund "…you'd be just as
well off if you'd invested in the S&P 500." *One Up on Wall Street*,
1989, p. 240.

Jonathan Clements, formerly *The Wall Street Journal*
"Most people can do it themselves. ... By indexing, you don't just
ensure that you will do better than most other investors. You will
also enjoy the advantage of 'relative certainty.' . . . For most
investors, Vanguard will be the place to go." *You've Lost It, Now
What? How to beat the bear market and still retire on time*, 2003,
p. 62, 70.

Charles D. Ellis, money managers' consultant
"The premise . . . that professional investment managers *can* beat
the market . . . appears to be false. It is a loser's game. ... clients
would have done better in a market fund." Returns are "splendidly
predictable—on average and over time." *Investment Policy, How
to Win the Loser's Game*, 1985, p. 5, 20, 34.

Jane Bryant Quinn, consumer advisor
"I'm a longtime booster of index mutual funds. These funds follow
the market as a whole. Tons of research has shown that most
money managers don't beat the markets they invest in, after costs.
Maybe your own stocks or funds have excelled in the past couple
of years. But in most cases, you've also been taking extra risk. The
odds of superior performance are against you, in the long run.

Indexing puts the odds on your side." *Los Angeles Business Journal*, May 8, 2000

Charles Schwab founder, discount broker
"I put my money where my mouth is: most of the mutual fund investments I have are in index funds, approximately 75%. My core investments are index funds. Experienced investors have discovered that in any given year, on average, only 20 to 30 percent of mutual funds outperform the market. That is why I recommend index funds…"
Mr. Schwab tells of one of his friends who owned many well-run funds. After keeping track of all the dividends, taxes, reinvestments tax basis and statements, he found he earned the same return as the index of these funds. After selling them all, he bought the index fund. He has "what he wanted in the first place: diversification, tax advantages, one statement, and lower expenses." *Guide to Financial Independence*, 1998, pp. 90, 103, 111.

Motley Fool, Internet site about investing
"Almost **everything** that you will ever read about mutual funds beyond, "Buy an index fund." is superfluous to your long-term success in investing in mutual funds." Fool.com.

Walter Updegrave, formerly senior editor, *Money*
"Mutual fund picking would be easier if there was one you could count on to outperform 70% or so of its competitors over long stretches of a decade or more. It's called an index fund. Although less than 10% of investors own an index fund, they are "one of the best-kept secrets" on Wall Street. My unabashed aim is to convince you to put at least a part of your money into one or more of these funds. You have a far less than a 50% chance of beating the market…. I strongly recommend that you make index funds your primary holding…." *The Right Way to Invest in Mutual Funds*, 1996, p 189-194.

Andrew Tobias, financial writer
"Scrimp and save, putting whatever you can into no-load, low-expense stock market index funds, both U.S. and foreign. You will

do better than 80% of your friends and neighbors." *My Vast Fortune*, 1997, p. 158.

There are many books written on the subject of index and "managed" funds. If you wish to vanquish the hype and understand investing, skim *A Random Walk Down Wall Street* by Princeton University's Burton Malkiel. Here are the reasons why smart insiders use low-cost funds:

1. Both stock and bond index funds provide better returns than 86% of managed funds for periods greater than 10 years.
2. You earn more because you pay lower costs and taxes.
3. Low-cost funds build greater wealth over time.
4. Low-cost funds can be less volatile because they reflect whole sectors of the market.
5. Low-cost funds offer better diversification.
6. You know what you are paying for. No high-salary managers.
7. Low-cost funds don't require you to hope the manager will predict the future correctly. The odds of doing it are 1 in 15,000 each year separately. Over time, all funds provide average returns minus their costs.
8. Low-cost funds are easy to buy.

> "Professional money management is a gigantic rip-off."
> Bill Gross, star bond manager, *Everything You've Heard About Investing is Wrong*

Summary of many studies about index investing

First, fund managers try to predict the future of the market when they buy and sell securities in their funds. There is no proof this can be done well over time. Yesterday's winners are usually tomorrow's losers. The AVERAGE market return has been 10-12%, so a few managers will beat the average by luck—Just not the same ones every year.
http://www.nytimes.com/2014/07/27/your-money/heads-or-tails-either-way-you-might-beat-a-stock-picker.html

Second, the costs of the manager, their staff and operations <u>must be paid for by you</u> whether or not they earn you a dime. It is always better to pay as little as possible for the same performance. <u>Costs can take 63% of our returns over time</u>. Surprisingly, while the stock index rose 10%, investors with high paid managers averaged only **3.79%** annually from 1982-2013 <u>DALBARinc.com</u>.

Third, high cost managers get paid for increasing the <u>size</u> of their funds, not for making you rich. Bringing in more money is a full-time job. It is expensive to market the funds given that there are now thousands available. It is inevitable that popular funds will grow until they produce average returns with high expenses. <u>Managers want to be rich</u>, not right.

Fourth, there is much less chance of you being treated poorly by fund management if the structure and governance are <u>customer-oriented</u> like Vanguard's and TIAA-CREF's are.

Fifth, many professional managers, pension funds, and Wall Street insiders place their core assets in low-cost index funds.

The best predictor of the success of a mutual fund is its cost. Why pay more than you have to? Usually the least expensive funds that match market averages beat the more expensive managed funds. Low-cost market index funds buy all the securities represented in a broad market. The goal of an index fund is to match its market. Low-cost index funds have provided returns that beat 80-90% of managed funds over the long-term. No manager has been able to predict the future so the returns regress to the mean—the 10%-12%. Wealthy people bet on the averages not the long shot. They don't like to lose value. The patient investor is rewarded in the long run. Buffett's **Wealth** strategy uses the simple plan of holding low-cost securities—either BRK in a discount broker or funds directly. Some clients use *Vanguard's Top Ten* inside a tax-FREE account.

> **"In every single time period and data point tested,
> low-cost funds beat high-cost funds."**

6

Hold profitable global companies

Join the Warren Buffett millionaire club!

If we want to have $1,000,000 for tax-FREE income later, we need a way to make it happen—a strategy. To be able to have a nest egg of $1 million requires that we know how and where to invest, invest regularly, invest properly, monitor accumulations along the way, and get help when we need it. We need a clear plan that takes only one hour to set up and only one hour per year to manage. Complicated plans just don't work for most people. Complicated strategies cost more to execute.

Picking *individual* stocks as a strategy is not likely to work for us. Professional managers and day traders have had limited success **over time**, unless they have insider information. Our strategy is to build wealth as a **silent partner** in growing global companies. Since it is unlikely that we (or anyone else) will be able to pick the next 'Apple,' we must invest in a group of firms. Buffett has purchased the best of the best at a discount. We don't have the skills to match his record. And we do not need to if we buy his holding company, Berkshire Hathaway (BRK.A or B).

However, if we fear owning just one stock, the alternative is to invest in a broad market index of the most successful ones. As the founder of the largest mutual fund firm, John Bogle, says: "Don't look for the needle. Buy the haystack."

This is contrary to the myth of Wall Street 'professionals.' They make their living claiming to find the needle every year and we pay the price. Professionals promise that they can find the next big one and we pay them well because we want to be rich. But....

Like the lottery, we kid ourselves into thinking that "someone has to win, why not me." We don't believe we are wasting our money even though our rational mind knows that our chance of winning is low. Managed funds don't beat the market over the long haul. The odds are like those of a lottery—18 million to 1. Like the lottery, when we invest in a managed fund to "beat the market" we don't count up all the costs of the "tickets." We may buy $25 worth of tickets a week and end up winning $1,000 in a year. But we spent $1,200 for $1,000.

In the same manner, a mutual fund manager advertises that their fund has "beaten" the market and so we pay 1-3% of our assets every year. Over time we find that while the stock market index rose about 11% a year from 1982-2013, we earned only 3.79% annually. This is what happened to retail investors according to Dalbar's QAIB recent study. DALBARinc.com

Some of us keep switching to the 'hot' funds according to the advertising we see. Some are always chasing the last successful mutual fund. Some buy the fund at the high point because they want the winner. They sell the fund when it falls and they want the next high flier. Over time they never earn the return promised by the manager. Past success is almost guaranteed future failure.

In this way, activity can take up to 63% of our returns over time. Each time we sell and buy, we give up earnings and perhaps part of our money if we use a sales person charging 5%. Even if we stay with one managed mutual fund that has annual fees of 1-3%, we are *killing the miracle of compounding*.

Using the compounding calculator, we can see that our accumulation drops to $0.7 million if we earn 10% instead of 12% annually. We could have $1 million in about 26 years at 11.5% using low-cost funds, no tax and no trading.
http://www.moneychimp.com/calculator/compound_interest_calculator.htm

Another Wall Street myth is that investing in market index funds will produce **only** average (mediocre) returns. It is true that the returns will be close to the returns of the market. However, historically the market returns are the ones that are somewhat predictable. However, historically the market returns (12%) are the ones that are somewhat predictable. Investing in an index provides no guaranteed return but the average returns have held steady since the 1950s. See the annual returns on page 32.

Wall Street's history is littered with strategies that were said to beat the market. The brilliant stock pickers have also come and gone (to the bank with fees). Today, though, which one of the new ones are we going to invest with? No one knows. The ONLY thing we really know is that the averages of broad market indexes have produced 10-12% each year. http://www.moneychimp.com/features/market_cagr.htm

For example, some of clients use these Vanguard mutual funds which have earned over 11% for a long time. Of course, there is no guarantee of future returns, but clients have done fairly well. Most started with the 500 Index and added companies in the Energy, Health and International sectors. These 10 funds have done well over time. Many investors pick Vanguard funds because the funds are well run 'at cost.' No "bells and whistles." No expensive managers and overhead. No owner or broker taking profits from our investment returns, even when there are none.

2013 Total Return	Fund	Long-term Return*	Longevity
32.3%	500 Index	11.0%*	since 1976
18.4%	Energy	13.2%	since 1984
38.4%	Extended Market	11.2%	since 1987
43.2%	Health	17.1%	since 1984
23.0%	International Growth	11.2%	since 1981
39.7%	PRIMECAP	13.7%	since 1984
37.6%	Small Cap Index	10.9%	since 1960
9.2%	Wellesley Income	10.1%	since 1970
36.1%	Windsor	11.6%	since 1958
30.7%	Windsor II	11.1%	since 1985
30.9%	Average	12.1%	

*Average Annual Returns as of 12/31/13.

These clients are patient long-term investors, not speculators. They believe that investments in low-cost funds (index and team-managed) are their best chance of reaching their goals. They have been rewarded for that belief. Vanguard has many low-cost funds and their customer service is better than most fund firms provide.

Remember, we are buying firms for the long-term. Most pension funds are invested in stock and bond indexes. Even though the market fell 22% in 2002 and jumped 29% in 2003, the average was still holding. Average returns mean we do not suffer the lowest lows nor the highest highs. Returns 'regress to the mean': 10-12%.

Most of the largest growing companies in the world are held by these funds. Large US firms are now earning at least **half of their**

profits overseas so we are benefiting from growth around the world. This is important because we don't want to miss important earnings progress as the developing nations like China and India expand their economies.

We don't know exactly which companies (Betamax) will be winners so we participate in all of them. We want to own some smaller growing companies too. If they become successful, they will move to the large company funds. We are exposed to almost all areas of the global economy by buying shares of these mutual funds at the lowest cost. We suffer the ups and downs of the markets just like every investor. However, we see that some funds do better at certain times while others do worse. Together we see clients hitting their goal of 10-12% average annual returns.

This type of investing has the greatest chance of avoiding severe swings in the balance of our accumulation. This type of strategy—investing in different types and sizes of companies in different sectors around the world—is called Modern Portfolio Theory. It is probably the best way to assure you of predictable retirement income too.

Modern Portfolio Theory

Some clients use the MPT strategy to control risk while increasing returns. MPT (Moneychimp.com/articles/risk/riskintro.htm) holds that if we put our eggs in different baskets of assets that grow at different times, then the value of all our 'eggs' grows with fewer ups and downs. We can manage the ups and downs of equity funds by buying different ones over time. Higher risk assets are small caps, REITs and foreign stocks. This strategy earns 10-12% with 30% less volatility.

Members assemble asset classes http://topforeignstocks.com/wp-content/uploads/2016/01/Callan-Periodic-Table-of-Investment-Returns-2015.png that fit their risk-reward tastes. According to this Nobel Prize-winning strategy moneychimp.com/articles/risk/portfolio.htm, a high return asset with a low correlation to other assets in the portfolio can actually reduce the volatility of the whole. It may be possible to earn high returns with less risk **overall** as each asset goes up and down at different times. See the example at

The past provides only PROBABLE futures. But isn't $1,000,000 (plus or minus $100,000) better than $150,000. Your $250/$500-per-month deposit in the bank for about 26 years will be worth about $156,000 compared with about $1 million from stock investing with no tax. Every investor would be better off with $1 million (+/- $100,000) than $156,000 from a bank.

Buffett has selected only the best firms in the economy at a discount so he is able to earn 20% a year not 11%. He owns companies in energy, insurance, staples, transport, jewelry, construction, tech, telecom, luxury, food, utilities, clothes, etc. http://www.berkshirehathaway.com/subs/sublinks.html

We can buy Buffett's companies as a share of his holding company, Berkshire Hathaway, BRK.A or B. B shares are mini version of A shares. In a discount brokerage, set up your share buying plan. Capital One makes it easy with the ShareBuilder Plan: https://www.capitaloneinvesting.com/main/investing/tools.aspx

You set up your Roth IRA account and fund it with a link to your checking account. You tell the trustee to debit $250 a month. BRK.B costs $140 3/12/16. You forget about it. You have no tax form to report and you don't need portfolio rebalancing. Let Buffett do his job. Look at your owner statement with patience.

Some clients prefer investing with mutual funds. You cannot buy *Vanguard's Top Ten* at once with $250 per month. Vanguard has minimums on all funds so they can keep their expenses low for everyone. They start with $1,000 in the STAR or Target 2060 fund.

There are two ways to start our fund account.
The easiest way is to save $250 a month in our savings account until we have the $1,000 minimum for Vanguard's entry fund: STAR #56. We can open the Roth IRA by phone or online: STAR minimum is $1,000. Most Vanguard funds need $3,000 to start. We can keep contributing to this index fund until we have $3,000 for the 500 Index and then $3,000 for the Extended Market funds. Vanguard is at 800.319.4254. STAR has returned 9.2% since 1985.

The second way to begin is to open a Roth IRA at TIAA, the world's largest pension company, primarily for educational and research institutions. Low expenses and low initial contributions make TIAA an organization we can stay with for life. Call TIAA at

800.842.2252.

At TIAA.org, we can make application and begin immediately with an automatic monthly contribution of $100 or more from our bank account. We can follow how the assets grow by themselves. TIAA has two funds that provide us with the diversity of companies worldwide: TIAA-CREF Equity Index and TIAA International Equity.

Request a *prospectus* (owner's manual) for each fund you will be using at Vanguard or TIAA. Both mutual fund firms have experienced salaried representatives that provide accurate information about accounts and funds. Both offer low-cost index funds that hold a broad representation of the market returns of 10-12%. This is a building block to accumulating wealth.

Both firms are focused on you, not on profits.

This simple strategy provides long-term returns of 10-12% annually on average with the benefit of avoiding single company or industry failures. It provides exposure to new growth potential around the world with less risk than holding one company, one sector, or one country. *The* **Vanguard Top Ten** *funds provide income, growth and diversification.*

Warren Buffett as your advisor has chosen the best of the best at a discount. His stock BRK.B provides you with income, growth and diversification. And his expertise provides you with the *peace of mind* of knowing you have the best advisor available. AND Warren may continue his 20% earnings phenomenon.

Join the Warren Buffett millionaire club!

7

Spend less than you earn

We need to find at least $250 per month to invest for the future. We can build wealth by following the strategy outlined in the previous chapters, but we need to have at least $250 available in the first place. In my experience, it doesn't matter how much people earn, most say they don't have the $250 a month to invest for their future. "Today is hard enough," they complain.

Yes, that may well be, but if we don't find the $250-$500 we won't be content tomorrow. We have to go back to our goal. We want to build wealth: accumulating $1,000,000 over time. Based on the way wealth compounds, we need to identify at least $250 a month on a permanent basis. We need to invest consistently or the miracle of compounding will not work.

No one wants to be restricted in their spending. And yet most people want to be content with their life. We must begin where we are. I have found that most people **don't mind saving $250** a month on expenses they don't need to make. In fact, they become proud of finding the wasted money. We use a *Spending Plan*.

If we consciously spend our income on those items on our priority list, we can't fail to develop the savings habit. We are teaching ourselves that **we can have whatever we want**, in time. We are not saying "no" to our desires. We are saying that all we want is on our list and we are working on our list. We will get what we want eventually. This is the only way to get a million dollars.

Our future is part of our immediate needs in the sense that if we don't prepare now, we won't have the future we want. Accumulating a $1,000,000 in a tax-FREE account is a lifelong process. It is like building a business: it takes patience. We follow the simple steps I explained above.

There are a number of ways to identify the $250 a month we

need to build our future. Some clients include the $250 in their automatic bill payment or have the trustee debit their account automatically. The contribution is just another bill like rent, mortgage, utilities, car payment, cable, phone, etc. They live on the balance of their income or borrow.

Others set up family goals and decide to put a certain amount in a separate account for each goal. In this way, they keep the wealth building process in the forefront of their monthly bill payments ritual. Others make investing automatic—out of sight.

Whatever way works for you. The important part is changing the status of wealth-building from a vague future to a monthly priority. **Making it automatic assures you that you will succeed**.

Most clients find that the easiest way is to set up an automatic debit of their checking account by the trustee at the time of the application for the Roth IRA. If we are using a Roth 401k or other employer account, we set up the retirement account with automatic contributions.

Your *Spending Plan* family agreement works for all goals: college fund, emergency fund, vacation fund, new *used* car fund, business start-up fund, whatever we decide to put at the top of our list of priorities. If we don't have this list, we can make one easily.

Clients who are successful have made written plans in some form or other. They have some idea of how much they will need at some time in the future. For short-term goals we can use our savings account but for long-term (5+ years) goals we need to use higher return mutual funds. Many clients have trouble deciding which investment to use for each goal.

I explained the chart we displayed on page 12 above. Stock mutual funds are the investment of choice for any long-term accumulation goal. As per the chart, annual returns of 10-12% are the norm for any accumulation over 5 years. Once we build up a sizable balance in a long-term account, we can "borrow" from ourselves for short-term needs as long as we pay ourselves back.

Thus, clients have used their long-term accumulation account for vacations, cars, appliances, emergencies, etc. This works if they pay themselves back. The account is set up as a Roth IRA so the *contributions* are not taxed when used before age 59.5. After that age, there are no taxes on earnings either—NEVER. However, to meet our long-term goals, we have to pay ourselves back quickly to take advantage of compounding. Compounding takes time.

Another benefit of using a Spending Plan is that we become focused on how we spend our money. We are more inclined to buy only what we need. For most of us, when we shop for groceries, we seek to get the most for our money by shopping for discounts and by buying in bulk. In the last ten years, the financial services industry has started to offer better values on products. We can avoid overpaying the middle people and buying products we really don't need. We can buy direct, without the middle person.

How can we buy direct? Our *Insiders Guides* provide an easy way to save $3,000 or more on financial products we already use. There are buyer's Guides for each specific area. We review some of the ways to find $250 in savings in the next chapter. http://www.amazon.com/Save-3000-every-year-Only/dp/1500681571

We can't build wealth by spending more than we earn. Building wealth takes patience and commitment to investing every month. This *Wealth* strategy is about simplicity and patience. We use the savings from paying less for the financial products we *really* need.

We direct the trustee to debit $250-$500 every month so *we can't fail* to create our tax-FREE $1,000,000 account.

Join the Warren Buffett millionaire club!

Are you paying too much?

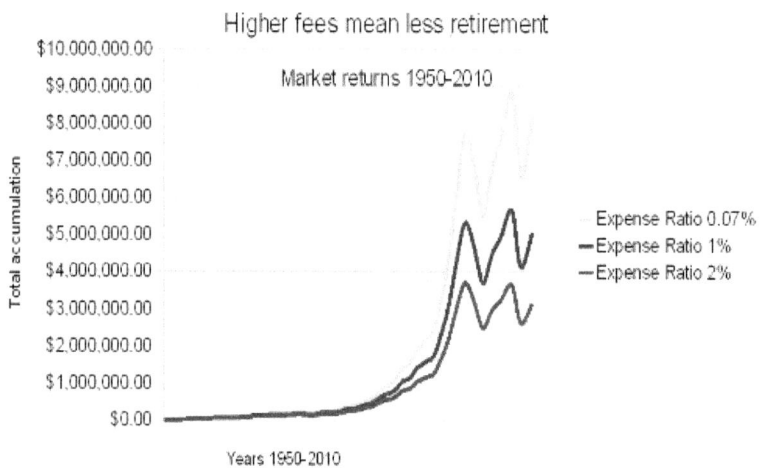

Higher fees mean less retirement

Market returns 1950-2010

Total accumulation

$10,000,000.00
$9,000,000.00
$8,000,000.00
$7,000,000.00
$6,000,000.00
$5,000,000.00
$4,000,000.00
$3,000,000.00
$2,000,000.00
$1,000,000.00
$0.00

Years 1950-2010

Expense Ratio 0.07%
—Expense Ratio 1%
—Expense Ratio 2%

8

Buy only what you need

It is easy to build wealth if we already have a pile of money. It takes 7-9 years to accumulate $1 million if we already have $500,000 in a mutual fund. But how do we capture that first $500,000, that first $250,000, or even that first $50,000? It comes from buying assets that 'grow by themselves.' It takes time and the easiest way to make sure we reach our goal is to make our monthly contributions automatic.

But where do we get the $250 or more? The best way is to "REDIRECT" the **cash we already spend** on things we really don't need or can buy for less. This can be your future:

Monthly	Accumulation at 12% per year									
	5	10	15	20	25	30	35	40	45	50
$100	$8,167	$23,004	$49,958	$98,925	$187,884	$349,496	$643,095	$1,176,477	$2,145,469	$3,905,834
$200	$16,334	$46,008	$99,916	$197,850	$375,768	$698,992	$1,286,190	$2,352,954	$4,290,938	$7,811,668
$300	$24,501	$69,012	$149,874	$296,775	$563,652	$1,048,488	$1,929,285	$3,529,431	$6,436,408	$11,717,502
$500	$40,835	$115,020	$249,790	$494,625	$939,420	$1,747,480	$3,215,475	$5,882,385	$10,727,346	$19,529,169

While working with clients, I have found that most of us waste $3,000 or more each year on financial services. We can stop paying for services we don't need. This takes a little thought and questioning on our part, but in reality it is the same process as buying any commodity. When we buy groceries, do we buy the house brand or the one on sale or the one we see advertised? On a little bigger scale, do we buy the new car advertised with a new "push" starter as opposed to a used car with a key? Do we pay an extra $1000 to buy the one with a PC screen to tell us where to go or just use our phone? The difference between paying full price for a new car and a 3-year-old model with fewer gadgets can be 40% or more. When we put our future on top of our priority list, we can REDIRECT the savings to a more worthwhile purpose.

It is the same with financial services. Most of us are not used to shopping for insurance, mutual funds, banking and mortgages. So we don't. We are operating under the mythology of Wall Street —'professionals' say we need them to help guide us, for a price. **But we don't need them anymore**. The world has changed.

Let's take some examples of <u>annual savings</u>:

Auto insurance: save $400 or more EVERY year by changing/dropping some extras we don't need.

Home insurance: save $200 or more EVERY year by changing one limit.

Life insurance: save $1,000 or more EVERY year by using direct to consumer insurer and low-cost term.

Mutual funds: save $2-3,000 EVERY year by using a low-cost provider.

Banking: save $120 EVERY year by using a low-cost provider of the benefits we usually use.

Mortgage: save $2,000 on closings and lower interest rates.

Investments: earn 15-30% guaranteed just by paying off credit cards too.

Tax refund: average $3,052 can pay for $1 million retirement.

Using the Insiders' Guides put together by Dan Keppel in his book ***The Insiders' Guides to Buying Discount Financial Services: Buy Direct and Save $3,000 Every Year,*** we can REDIRECT the $250 a month without having to give up anything important. We don't need to 'tighten our belts' or make a budget. We can give up things we would not benefit from anyway.

Dan gave me a number of testimonials from people who have told him about their experience using the Guides.

George B. New York:
"I saved $1,356 on my vehicle insurance using your Insider's Guide to Vehicle Insurance. I saved by using some of your Insiders' 'tricks of the trade' like dropping the extras that I already had."

John D. New York:
"I canceled my life insurance and used the money to buy the

mutual funds. You were right. I didn't need the insurance anymore. My kids are all grown. My new wife and I invest as much as we can now. Your Guide to 'Living' Insurance is a great way to look at our insurance needs."

Mark K. Ohio:
"I had no idea how to invest in the 401k that my new job offered. I have not been disappointed with the mutual funds suggested by other members. I saved about a $1,000 by transferring my old 401k mutual funds to the low-cost funds in your Guide. When I sold my primary residence in 2004, I followed members' advice with the gains. I use all your Guides to help me save more for my retirement since I got a late start. Thanks."

Dan has a great example of the big savings we can expect by shopping for insurance. Dan found that people usually pick name brands instead of shopping. Companies spend a lot for TV advertising and gimmicks that cost you.

Example from 2010:

MetLife charged $983 for a $300,000 30-year **term policy**. This same $300,000 benefit was sold by Savings Bank Life Insurance for $384 a year. Their financial strength ratings are A+ and their underwriting requirements are the same. The difference, $599, over 30 years is $17,970. If invested, this difference can add $175,000 to OUR **account**.

Most people are amazed at the difference a little research and shopping can accomplish. Even if we did not have Dan's Guides, a search of the Internet would reveal several portals that quote rates. Unfortunately, most people don't take the time to shop or don't know exactly what they need. The Guides help us make the decision of where to shop and what to buy.

Buying only what we need in every financial service area will provide the cash for contributions to our wealth. Taking the time to shop in each area of our expenses helps us make our future happen. Shopping for an hour can add $175,000 to our account. Yes, it is worth it! The bright future starts with every $250 invested in Warren Buffett's stock or low-cost mutual funds.

The Roth IRA Rules

Contributions:

$5,500 ($6,500 over age 50) each year
Income under $132,000 (2016) single
married $194,000 (2016)

Distributions:

Tax-FREE for contributions.
And Tax-FREE for earnings if
Over age 591/2,
Account open 5 years,
Earnings are taxable if under age, unless
Disabled, or
First home ($10,000), or
Death

Bonus:

Account can grow tax-FREE for life
Distribution rules don't apply
Heirs don't pay income tax
Account has no maximum

Check with your tax preparer
https://www.irs.gov/pub/irs-pdf/p590a.pdf

9

Manage the account once a year

We continue to make more money when *snoring* than when active.

Warren Buffett, Berkshirehathaway.com/

This is the advice of the most successful investor of our day. He is making it clear that we should NOT touch our investments very often. Contrary to the advice of the Wall Street 'professionals,' he **leaves his assets alone** to compound over time. He does not follow the 'hot' investment of the day. He buys the stock of growing companies around the world. He has held some investments for over 40 years—Coke, GEICO, AmEx, WellsFargo, DairyQueen.

Our emotions tell us to sell when our account balance goes down. We want to buy the next investment 'hit' to make up for previous losses. This is why we have a hard time following Buffett's advice. However, the emotions that cause us to be bad investors are what we can control—not the stock price of growing companies worldwide. Patience is a habit we can learn.

Our contributions to our account need to be automatic so we **buy more shares when the market is down** and less when it is up. This helps us control our emotions. When the market is down, we need to look at the line graph on page 13. We don't know when the market will be up or down but we see that if we sell, we may miss the next advance. This is why we have to remember Warren Buffett's advice and hold on to stocks forever. In fact, Mr Buffett says **"our favorite holding period is forever."**
http://www.berkshirehathaway.com/letters/1988.html

When we own a broad cross-section of the market, we really **don't have to worry** about buying and selling our mutual funds. There is no better investment for the long term. Besides, what would we buy if we sold? We have seen that stocks are the safest investment for periods over 10 years. Patience is profitable.

We believe that the only way to avoid bad investment decisions is to NOT make any investment decisions in haste. Stick with the idea that we only have to look at our tax-FREE account once a year. At that time, I make sure I am making contributions to the specific mutual fund I need to build in order to keep the balance equal. I don't sell because there is no safer investment.

For instance, when I first started investing, I used the 500 Index. After I had accumulated enough to buy the Extended Market Idx, I sold shares of 500 Index ($3,000) and bought it. I kept investing into the 500 Index until I had the minimum for the next one on the list. I repeated this pattern until I had the minimum in each. Then I picked one to add $250 a month for one year. The next year, I did the same until I completed the list again and again.

Today, I am still making contributions using the same rotation. Once a year, I compare the total account balance to where I think it should be. I note what happened during the year for any one fund. I read about that Vanguard fund. Do I need to make a change? No, usually I don't. I use the 10 funds listed above. They have consistently done well over the years.

Notice that when we buy each fund at first, we have to sell shares in the 500 Index to do so. Because we are using a Roth IRA, there is no tax on this transfer if the share price has gone up. Also, each year, our dividends are re-invested without paying tax on that income. This is part of the miracle of compounding. Our account is growing without taxes each year. Any other non-retirement account would be diminished by the tax paid each year.

There is no need to sell funds that have done well in order to re-balance the 10 funds' balances equally. Most of the research shows that re-balancing each year does not change the long-term outcome of the whole portfolio. Some clients use their contributions each year to add to the fund that has grown the **least**. However, as each fund becomes larger, the effect of adding contributions becomes smaller over time.

When we have to sell shares to meet an emergency or avoid interest payments by using cash for large ticket items, we may sell shares in each fund by equal dollar amounts. This is a better strategy than selling shares in only one fund since we don't know which fund may recover the fastest going forward. In the same way as accumulating shares, we need to reimburse our account for the amount used. It is very desirable to also continue to make contributions at the regular rate—$250-$500 per month. This way we are assured of catching up to our position as we reach our goal.

However, we found that after accumulating a large proportion of our goal, making contributions did not seem to matter to the outcome. For instance, the client whose account is shown on page 22 took $25,000 for a used luxury car in the year the account hit over half a million. He also stopped making contributions. His account total did not suffer in the long run.

Actually this client redirected his $250 monthly contribution to his grandchild's Roth IRA so that they might have a financial foundation all their life. If he keeps giving this $3,000 a year to his offspring for 30 years, they could have $1,000,000 by age 50. The grandchild "earns" $3,000 a year doing odd jobs for him. Learn more about this "Gift of a Lifetime" in Dan Keppel's book, amazon.com/Give-your-Grandchild-2,000,000-Lifetime/.

Our tax-FREE retirement income account does not require us to hire an advisor to manage it. **We have Buffett**. Advisors do not know what the future holds anymore than we do so paying them 1-3% each year just reduces our annual returns. Their fees/charges can take up to 63% of our total accumulations over time. We are investing for the long term and there is proof that switching from one fund to another only hurts our results. As we add more contributions, we own more Berkshire Hathaway or can rotate through each fund if we use *Vanguard's Top Ten*. The less we tamper with our fund balances the better our experience will be. Remember, we are patient silent partners in growing businesses around the world.

This is how we create wealth.

Join the Warren Buffett millionaire club!

Your Action Plan
This is our plan for *Wealth:*

This week:

Goal
Set up Roth IRA and start automatic contributions with trustee

This month:
Goal
Do nothing with investments

Next month:
Goal
Do Nothing with investments

This year:
Goals
Check fund totals and redirect automatic contributions if necessary

2nd year:
Goals
Check fund totals and redirect automatic contributions if necessary

3rd year:
Goals
Check fund totals and redirect automatic contributions if necessary

4th year:
Goals
Check fund totals and redirect automatic contributions if necessary

Every year:
Goals
Check fund totals and redirect automatic contributions if necessary

10

Take $80,000 tax-FREE a year in retirement

We have purchased BRK.B stock through ShareBulder or invested in **Vanguard's Top Ten** funds. We have learned to be **patient** and accumulate $1,000,000 or more the **simple** way. We have paid back any amounts that we borrowed to avoid paying interest. We have been **fortunate** that the historical averages of market returns have produced the accumulations we set as our goals.

NOW WHAT?

Now we can take $80,000 (8%) out of the accounts each year and pay no income taxes. Most states follow the IRS code on our Roth IRA—§ 408 trust account. *No state tax.*
http://www.irs.gov/retirement/article/0,,id=137307,00.html
Some clients have shifted some of their accumulations into the **Wellesley Income** fund in order to provide a monthly income to their checking account. They created a *retirement spending plan* that assured them of that monthly income of a fixed dollar amount with this Guide: amazon.com/Your-Retirement-Spending-Plan-enough.
We have to create our $1,000,000 nest egg in order to provide the same buying power as we have today because of inflation. I am assuming that most families will need at least $40,000 (current dollars) a year to live on in retirement. We don't know what will happen to Social Security by 2034. We don't know what employer pensions might look like by then. I am assuming that inflation will continue at a 3% rate. It might be more or less. I have no idea. However, we must prepare for inflation.
At 3%, inflation will make the goods we now buy for $40,000 cost about $80,000. This is not exact. I don't know what will happen in 30 days let alone 30 years. If Social Security or

employer pensions can provide our basic income, that is fine. But we don't want to count on them. We need to grow our account.

I am using $40,000 as a basic needs income because that has been my experience of what working people desire. It is also an amount that could be generated for life by our $1,000,000 account balance. Many clients use 7%-8% as a target for their investment returns in retirement. This is just an approximation of the average returns over time. Our *Vanguard Top 10* provide over 10%.

Some clients transfer some of their money into a balanced fund like the **Wellesley Income** in order to generate the income for the coming year. The balance of their tax-FREE account remains in the broad market funds we have listed above. These funds may continue to produce returns in the 10-12% range. If there is a bad year like 2008, we are not taking money out of our principal at a bad time. We take the money from the Wellesley Income fund with 60% income-earning bonds.

The funds we have listed above include some of the most consistent low volatility returns over time. The **Wellesley Income** fund has produced over 10% per year on average since 1970. It contains stocks and bonds. **This fund alone might be our source** of annual withdrawals of interest and dividends. Since our **account** is not taxable, there are no tax considerations in the decision of which fund to tap for our monthly income.

Buffett has suggested his executor use a bond fund for income. http://www.berkshirehathaway.com/letters/2013ltr.pdf p 20.

Because we have no tax liability on this real income $3,333 per month, we may not have to pay tax on our other income like Social Security and/or our qualified retirement funds. 85% of Social Security benefits are currently subject to federal income taxes. Typically those with little or no other taxable income currently have no tax due on their Social Security benefits. Pensions, 401k, IRAs, and annuities are taxed as *earned* income since we did not pay tax on the contributions (or most of them).

In most cases, we will pay little income tax on our income in retirement since the bulk of it, $80,000 ($40,000 adjusted for inflation), will be tax-FREE. This will give us 25-30% more cash to spend compared with others who have taxable income. Pensions and other taxable income may be taxed at even higher rates in the future to pay for the two wars and two tax cuts since 2001. (America has never gone to war and taken tax breaks at the same time before so this will take time to pay off.)

Our tax-FREE income will provide us with most of our needs. If we continue to follow the same **Wealth** strategy, we will find a comfortable lifestyle throughout the 30 to 40 years of not working unless we want to.

I and many clients are assuming we will work at least part time after we take full retirement and begin collecting Social Security. If benefits are cut, we will need to work. We are encouraged to use our tax-FREE income to develop a small business since this can help us control the income that is taxed.

As I mentioned at the beginning of this book, many working millionaires are self-employed. Running a small business is a great way to control the taxes we pay. Taxes are the biggest killer of wealth-building. It destroys the compounding factor.

The accumulation of $1,000,000 over time can be achieved with patience and perseverance. Spending the income that $1,000,000 can generate may require us to take some principal from time to time. If we use the same wealth building strategy to do this, we will probably have enough to take care of long-term health care and other unforeseen expenses. Since we don't know what may happen, we will want to continue the same habits we have developed before retirement. We live within our means.

We may find that we will have a sizable legacy as we age. There are many ways to pass on our wealth that don't require attorney fees and complicated legal formulations. Many clients have found that incremental gifts to charity and family provide immediate gratification. They have used the suggestions for wealth transfer Dan Keppel presented in the *Retirement Spending Plan*.
amazon.com/Your-Retirement-Spending-Plan-enough/dp/1461084016/

Our special investment account is tax-FREE and can have the purchasing power of about $40,000 in today's dollars. They travel and share with family. Most continue to earn income doing what they enjoy or provide help to others in their volunteer efforts. Our nest egg and all the earnings are TAX-FREE.

Mr Buffett's stock has made us millionaires.

How to Buy Securities For Retirement

1. Cost matters: Full Service Broker/advisor cost 1% to 3%

If you use a salesperson, fees can cost HALF A NEST EGG!
$6,000 per year @11% for 28 years = $1,064,740
$6,000 per year @11-1% for 28 years = $885,795
$6,000 per year @11-2% for 28 years = $738,807
$6,000 per year @11-3% for 28 years = $617,570

2. Broker/advisor stock picking does not beat index funds over the long run. No money manager has been able to beat the market over time except Warren Buffett who holds the company forever.

3. Time is the key to investment success. The chance of you buying AND selling, both, at the right times, is near zero.

4. A Tax-FREE investment account increases your balance 25%.

5. Putting all your money in one stock or market sector guarantees failure over time. No one investment is perfect. Buffett's BRK owns many firms in many sectors so it's like a stock index fund.

6. 'Dollar cost average' buying technique lowers the cost of shares over time. When you invest a fixed amount each month, you buy more shares when the price is low and less when high. Over time, you will own more shares at a lower average cost.

7. If you don't have years to retirement, convert part of your 401k or IRA to a Roth IRA each year, paying tax as you go.

8. Market down? Look at Tom's account balances again, p. 22. Hold on! Buffett's holding period is **forever** too.

"We make more money when *snoring*"

Join the Warren Buffett millionaire club!

It is hard to be patient and leave your money alone to grow by itself. Most people don't have the experience with a business or investing in companies that grow. They don't see the market the way that Warren Buffett does. They see it as a casino where the lucky win or a black hole where speculators lose their life savings.

Warren Buffett sees it as a place where the patient ones take money from those who panic. Investors in Buffett's Berkshire Hathaway have seen increases of 20% a year—doubling every 3.5 years—because they held shares even when there was a <u>loss</u>.

The impatient stock trader would have seen an increase of only 3.79% from buying and selling. 3.79%—hardly more than inflation! If you knew anything about investing, you would have put your money in Buffett's holding company. All his stocks tanked for a while but the person who did nothing is now wealthy. Their <u>$40 might be worth $10,000,000 now</u>.

Most of us do not know which businesses will grow quickly in the future. We have to "settle" for the average returns of 10-12% a year. Each of our $3,000 investments would be worth about $30,000 over 20 years in a diversified group of businesses like those in *Vanguard's Top Ten* above. For instance, Vanguard's low-cost Health Care Fund has provided <u>17% a year since 1984</u>.

Most of us know we will never be able to pick the right companies for the future. Wall Street tempts us by claiming they know. Some of us follow their advice and pay dearly. The industry tells us that *we need them* to make money. They take <u>$560 billions</u> year after year but we earn only 3.79% on average. Trading stocks does NOT benefit us. <u>pbs.org/moyers/journal/09282007/</u>

A person paying 1-3% of their nest egg every year to an advisor can't then admit they get very little for their money. Most advisors can't beat the investment return of the market so that $3-5,000 a year in fees is wasted—just paying the <u>Wall Street Wolf</u>.

Over time that fee goes up and can take up to <u>63%</u> of our total possible accumulations. Advisors like to buy and sell securities creating taxes and commissions that don't help us. Large pensions don't buy and sell. <u>businessweek.com/articles/2013-01-24/</u>

The **key** to reaching our goal of $1,000,000 is *compounding* of high returns over time. If we pay 2% to earn 10-12%, we net 8-10%. Since we know that no advisor can guarantee 10-12% and most studies show investing directly without a "professional" can yield a better result, there is no reason to give up 2%. Advisors usually charge 1-3% whether they beat the averages or not so it is better to go for the 10-12% on our own. Sales people don't give refunds if they don't beat the market!

The clear **winning strategy** is to do nothing but buy and hold high-earning securities and let compounding work its miracle. Buffett holds the best firms at a discount forever and proves this strategy works. Over time using a tax-FREE account with low costs, we can accumulate enough from $250 a month. Using a compounding calculator <u>http://www.moneychimp.com/ calculator/compound_interest_calculator.htm</u>, we find the range is about 22 years for Buffett's BRK. If each spouse has an account, we can be assured of enough income no matter how long we live.

If we use an advisor, we may give up over $350,000 in total accumulation. Research has shown that the average brokerage investor actually earns about **3.79%** annually, (1982-2015 QAIB <u>DALBARinc.com</u>), NOT the market rate of 10-12%.

Our approach to building **Wealth** works because it employs a simple strategy using a unique **tax-FREE trust account** that eliminates the biggest killer of wealth: TAXES. We have seen that compounding over time is the real engine for building wealth. Most people are NOT going to be successful at this because they are impatient and don't let compounding do the work. Plus they pay high fees. Holding BRK in a discount broker costs much less.

We will never be taxed on this money—it is like Uncle Sam "giving" us $350,000! We avoid the 25% Fed and 5-7% tax of most states on income from our $1 million account.

We can be our own masters of tax-FREE income with patience. There is no need to pick individual stocks or hire expensive advisors or product pushers with hidden fees. We can do it

ourselves with our simple strategy—hold BRK or *Vanguard's Top Ten*. All we need to do is put our investment plan on automatic and then do NOTHING. Buffett has proved this strategy with thousands of millionaires and billionaires from all walks of life.
http://www.wsj.com/articles/warren-buffetts-lucky-millionaires-club-1445419800

You must take the first step. Call ShareBulder 877-595-0014 or Vanguard 800-551-8631 or TIAA 800-842-2252 yourself to set up your accounts. It takes about an hour to set up a Roth IRA for both of you. You can do it online or by phone with a licensed rep. Put the contributions on automatic so you don't have to decide whether to invest. You can't fail. Life happens and there is always an emergency that requires cash. But future life happens too and you want to be spending your $6,666 a month, $80,000 a year; not praying Washington won't cut your Social Security benefits.

There is a clear reason why we become wealthy. It is not luck or inheritance. Millions of immigrants to this country have done it before. They lived below their means. They saved and invested in businesses they worked. They did not let temporary cash flow problems stop them from building wealth. They used the Buffett strategy by any other name, every day. As many clients say,

"I never even miss the contributions because I never see them. Then all of a sudden, I see my statement" [has $25,000, $50,000, $250,000, $1,000,000.] "We are talking real money here."
Join the Warren Buffett millionaire club!

http://www.thestreet.com/online-trading/compare-best-online-brokers.html

Call ShareBulder 877.595.0014 today
https://www.capitaloneinvesting.com/main/investing/tools.aspx

Call Vanguard 800.551.8631 today
https://investor.vanguard.com/what-we-offer/iras/traditional-iras-and-roth-iras

or TIAA-CREF 800.842.2888 today.
https://www.tiaa.org/public/pdf/mfirains.pdf

NOTES

Priorities	Time-line
Retirement $1 million	22 years
_____	_____
_____	_____
_____	_____
_____	_____
_____	_____

It is the amount we KEEP that matters!

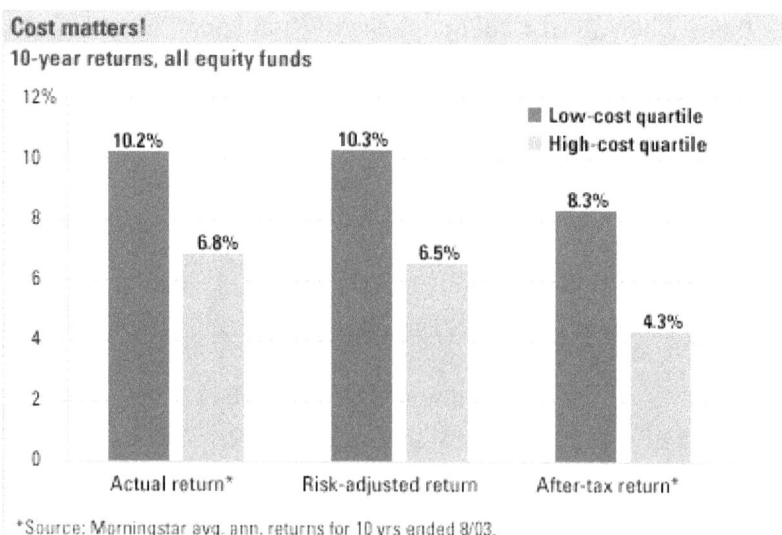

Cost matters!
10-year returns, all equity funds

- Low-cost quartile
- High-cost quartile

Actual return*: 10.2% / 6.8%
Risk-adjusted return: 10.3% / 6.5%
After-tax return*: 8.3% / 4.3%

*Source: Morningstar avg. ann. returns for 10 yrs ended 8/03.

The Author

Zhou Wang has been in financial services for over 20 years. He was a managing executive of the sales units of a number of firms. He is one of the insiders who contributed to the *The Insiders Guides* set of buyers' guides edited by Dan Keppel. The guides provide specific ways to save on all financial services. ***The Insiders' Guides to Buying Discount Financial Services: Buy Direct and Save $3,000 Every Year*** is available at Amazon, Barnes & Noble, Junglee, bookadda, allbookstores, ebay, fishpond, alibris, powells, booksamillion, etc

To receive a weekly Alert with wealth-building ideas, go to www.TheInsidersGuides.com

www.ingramcontent.com/pod-product-compliance
Lightning Source LLC
Chambersburg PA
CBHW070354190526
45169CB00003B/1015